The Power of Influence

Unseen Social Forces

JD ARDEN

Preface

We like to think of ourselves as individuals—unique, self-determined, and independent in our thoughts and actions. But beneath the surface, we are influenced by countless unseen forces, shaping our behaviors, our choices, and even our sense of identity. These forces are not overt or easily identifiable. They are the subtle currents of social expectation, the quiet whispers of authority, the unspoken cues that move us in one direction or another, often without our conscious awareness.

In *The Power of Influence: Unseen Social Forces*, we explore how deeply these invisible forces infiltrate our lives. From the pressures of social media validation to the insidious ways cultural norms dictate who we think we should be, this book is an invitation to look beneath the surface and understand what truly drives us. The influence of those around us is inevitable—whether it's a parent, a peer, or an algorithm feeding us information. But what we do with that influence, how we respond to it, and whether we allow it to shape our lives without question—that is up to us.

This book isn't just about identifying the forces at play. It's about empowerment. It's about arming ourselves with the knowledge to make conscious choices, to resist manipulation, and to reclaim autonomy in a world that constantly tries to tell us who to be. As you journey through these chapters, my hope is that you will gain a deeper understanding of the forces that shape you, so that you can navigate them with clarity and intention.

We cannot escape influence, nor should we want to. Influence is part of being human, part of connecting with others, part of belonging to something bigger than ourselves. But we can learn to see it, to understand it, and ultimately, to use it in ways that serve us, rather than control us. Let's step into the unseen together, uncover what lies beneath, and take back the power to define our own lives.

Chapter 1: The Hidden Currents of Influence

Influence often operates like an undercurrent, invisible but powerful enough to shape the direction of our lives. We walk through our days assuming that we are the masters of our own choices, believing in the autonomy of our thoughts and the clarity of our decisions. But beneath the surface, unseen forces are at play—gently nudging us, shaping our behaviors, and moulding our beliefs without our explicit consent. These forces are not dramatic, not loud; they are subtle, constant, and, because of that, incredibly effective.

From the moment we are born, we are immersed in a sea of influences. Parents, teachers, friends, society, and even the culture we are born into—all contribute to the person we become. These are not always conscious lessons, not always taught in words. Instead, they are absorbed through the quiet acts of observation, imitation, and the instinctive desire to fit in and belong. Influence is in the tone of a parent's voice when they express approval or disapproval, in the casual habits of a friend group, in the advertisements that paint a picture of what a happy life should look like. It is everywhere, and it is constant.

The truth is, humans are social creatures. We thrive on connection, on community, and, as a result, we are wired to be influenced by those around us. This is not inherently bad—in fact, it's a survival mechanism. Our ancestors learned what was safe to eat, where to find shelter, and how to survive from others in their community. This ability to learn, to adapt, and to follow the cues of the group is what allowed humans to thrive. But the very mechanism that kept us safe in the past can also lead us to make decisions that are not always in our best interest today. We are influenced not just by those we trust, but by those who may have their own interests at heart—marketers, politicians, social media influencers, and countless others who know exactly how to tap into the currents of influence.

One of the most significant hidden currents of influence is the desire to belong. The need to be accepted by others is one of the most powerful motivators in human behavior. It shapes what we wear, how we speak, what we believe, and even how we perceive ourselves. The fear of rejection—of being seen as different or not fitting in—can lead us to make choices that are not in line with our true desires or values. We conform, often unconsciously, to the expectations of the group, even when those expectations do not serve us. This is how influence works—not through force, but through the gentle pressure to fit in, to be one of the crowd.

Another hidden current of influence is the power of repetition. The more we hear something, the more likely we are to believe it. This is a principle that has been understood for centuries, used by everyone from political leaders to advertisers. Repetition creates familiarity, and familiarity breeds acceptance. The more a message is repeated, the more it becomes embedded in our minds, until we start to accept it as truth—often without questioning its origins or validity. This is why propaganda works, why advertising is effective, and why certain cultural narratives become ingrained in society. The power of repetition is a subtle but relentless force, shaping our beliefs over time without us even noticing.

The influence of authority is another hidden force that shapes our behavior. We are conditioned to trust authority figures, to follow their lead, to assume that they know best. From early childhood, we learn to obey parents, teachers, and other figures of authority. This conditioning continues into adulthood, where we find ourselves trusting experts, following leaders, and often complying with instructions without questioning them. Authority can be a force for good—it can provide guidance, wisdom, and structure. But it can also be exploited, leading us to make choices that serve the interests of the authority rather than our own.

The subtlety of influence is what makes it so powerful. Unlike overt coercion, which is easily recognized and resisted, influence works beneath the surface. It shapes our perceptions, our preferences, our sense of what is normal or desirable. It works through the people we trust, the culture we are part of, the media we consume. And because it is subtle, we often do not even realize that we are being influenced. We believe that our choices are our own, that our beliefs are formed independently, that our preferences are purely personal. But in truth, much of who we are and what we do is shaped by the hidden currents of influence.

The purpose of this chapter is not to suggest that influence is inherently bad—it is not. Influence is a natural part of being human. It is what connects us to others, what allows us to learn and grow, what gives us a sense of belonging. But it is important to understand that influence is always present, always at work, and that if we are not aware of it, we risk losing control over our own lives. The key is awareness—recognizing when we are being influenced, understanding how that influence works, and making conscious choices about whether to accept or resist it.

In the chapters that follow, we will explore the various forms of unseen social influence, from the powerful pull of peer pressure to the impact of social media algorithms. We will learn how to identify these forces, how they shape us, and how we can take back control. Influence is everywhere, but with awareness, it does not have to control us. By understanding the hidden currents that shape our lives, we can learn to navigate them with intention, making choices that are truly our own.

Chapter 2: The Pull of the Tribe: Social Conditioning and Belonging

The need to belong is an ancient instinct, as vital to human survival as food and shelter. For our ancestors, belonging to a group meant safety, access to resources, and support against the harsh realities of the natural world. This instinct for connection runs deep, and even today, in our hyper-individualistic modern society, the pull of the tribe continues to shape our choices and behaviors. We may believe that our actions are entirely our own, that our beliefs are a product of independent thought, but beneath it all lies the quiet, often unnoticed, pressure of social conditioning—the influence of the tribe that we have been part of since birth.

From the earliest days of life, we are molded by the expectations and behaviors of those around us. As infants, we learn to mimic our parents' facial expressions, sounds, and gestures. This instinct to imitate is the first step in social conditioning—a mechanism through which we begin to absorb the unspoken rules of belonging. We grow up being taught not only how to walk and talk but also what is considered good, bad, desirable, and taboo. These lessons are not always explicit. Many of them come from watching how our parents react to a situation, from the approval we receive for certain actions, and the subtle disapproval for others. By the time we reach adolescence, we have already internalized countless norms, behaviors, and values, all of which shape how we perceive ourselves and the world.

One of the most powerful forces in social conditioning is conformity—the tendency to align our attitudes, beliefs, and behaviors with those of the group. Conformity is a natural response to the desire to belong, to avoid conflict, and to maintain social harmony. As social creatures, we are wired to minimize friction within our group because harmony means security. This is why we find ourselves laughing at jokes we don't find funny, agreeing with opinions we don't fully understand, and even adopting habits we may not entirely believe in. Conformity can be as simple as wearing the same style of clothing as our friends or as profound as adopting cultural or religious beliefs that shape our worldview.

The power of social conditioning is especially apparent during adolescence. This stage of life is marked by a heightened need to belong, as the instinct to form social connections becomes critical to our identity. Adolescents often find themselves torn between the desire to express individuality and the fear of standing out too much—of being ostracized by their peers. The opinions of friends, the fear of being seen as different, and the desire for acceptance all combine to create a powerful pull that can shape everything from fashion choices to academic interests, from hobbies to the values that guide their lives. It is during this time that many of the foundational aspects of our social identity are solidified, often without us realizing how much influence the tribe has had in their formation.

Social conditioning extends far beyond adolescence. As adults, we continue to be influenced by the norms and expectations of the groups we belong to—whether it is our family, our workplace, our community, or even the broader culture. These groups each have their own set of values, standards, and behaviors that dictate what is acceptable and what is not. The culture we grow up in plays a significant role in shaping how we view success, relationships, gender roles, and even happiness. For instance, in some cultures, success is measured by personal achievement and wealth, while in others, it is defined by community well-being and family connections. These cultural values become ingrained in us, not because we consciously choose them, but because they are the water we swim in—the invisible backdrop against which we measure our lives.

The desire to belong can also lead us to suppress parts of ourselves that do not align with the expectations of our tribe. We may hide our true opinions, downplay our interests, or even mask aspects of our personality in order to fit in. This can lead to a kind of internal dissonance—a sense that we are not living authentically because we are constantly adjusting ourselves to meet the expectations of others. The fear of rejection, of being cast out of the group, is a powerful motivator. It pushes us to conform, even when that conformity comes at the cost of our own happiness and authenticity.

The influence of social conditioning is not always negative. It provides structure, a sense of identity, and a framework within which we learn how to interact with others. The norms and values of the tribe can guide us toward positive behaviors—kindness, cooperation, respect for others. But it can also be limiting. When social norms become rigid, when they dictate that there is only one acceptable way to live, they can stifle individuality and creativity. They can prevent us from questioning harmful traditions, from challenging outdated beliefs, and from exploring paths that may be more aligned with who we truly are.

One of the most profound ways in which social conditioning manifests is through the concept of "social roles." These are the expectations placed on us based on factors like gender, age, profession, or social status. From a young age, we are conditioned to understand what is expected of us— how boys should behave versus how girls should behave, what it means to be a "good" student, a responsible adult, a caring parent. These roles are deeply ingrained, and stepping outside of them often comes with social repercussions. A woman who chooses not to have children, for example, or a man who decides to be a stay-at-home father, may face judgment not because of the intrinsic value of their choices but because they have stepped outside of the roles that society has assigned to them. These roles are part of the fabric of the tribe—they provide order, predictability, and a sense of identity—but they can also be restrictive, preventing individuals from pursuing a life that truly reflects their desires and values.

The key to navigating the pull of the tribe is awareness. We cannot escape social conditioning—it is a fundamental part of being human. But we can become aware of the forces at play, recognize when we are conforming out of fear rather than genuine desire, and choose consciously which aspects of the tribe we want to embrace and which we want to question. This requires a willingness to stand out, to risk being different, and to accept that not everyone will approve of our choices. It requires courage—the courage to be ourselves even when it means stepping outside of the norms that have shaped us.

Breaking free from negative aspects of social conditioning is not about rejecting the tribe entirely. It is about finding a balance—embracing the positive aspects of connection and belonging while refusing to be confined by expectations that do not serve us. It is about recognizing that while we are shaped by our environment, we also have the power to shape ourselves, to decide which influences we accept and which we resist. This is not an easy path. It requires introspection, honesty, and a willingness to face the discomfort that comes with stepping outside of the familiar. But it is the only way to live authentically, to create a life that is truly our own rather than one that has been dictated by the invisible forces of social conditioning.

In the next chapter, we will explore another powerful force of influence— the authority effect. We will examine why we are wired to obey authority figures, how this instinct has been both a source of strength and a vulnerability, and how understanding the dynamics of authority can help us make more conscious choices in our lives. The pull of the tribe may shape our identity, but the commands of authority can direct our actions, often in ways we do not fully understand. Understanding these forces is key to navigating the unseen currents that influence our lives.

Chapter 3: The Authority Effect: Why We Obey

Authority is one of the most powerful unseen forces that shape human behavior. From early childhood, we are conditioned to respect and follow authority figures—parents, teachers, community leaders, and eventually bosses, government officials, and experts in various fields. This conditioning is not accidental; it is deeply ingrained in our biology and psychology. Authority offers structure, safety, and direction, making it an essential component of societal function. But the same instinct that allows us to learn and grow under the guidance of authority can also lead us to act against our better judgment, sometimes even against our values.

To understand why we obey, we must first explore the roots of authority. Historically, authority played a critical role in human survival. In primitive societies, following the leader—usually the strongest, the wisest, or the most experienced—meant a greater chance of survival for the group. Leaders made decisions about when to hunt, where to find water, and how to protect against threats. Those who followed survived, while those who did not often faced dire consequences. This evolutionary pressure led to a deep-seated inclination to defer to authority, an instinct that remains with us today.

The famous experiments by Stanley Milgram in the 1960s provide a striking example of how powerful the authority effect can be. Milgram's study showed that ordinary people were willing to administer what they believed were painful electric shocks to another person simply because an authority figure—wearing a lab coat and presenting themselves as an expert—instructed them to do so. The participants' discomfort was evident, but most continued to obey, even when it conflicted with their personal morals. This experiment demonstrated that the authority effect can override empathy, ethical beliefs, and common sense. It showed that under the right conditions, the pull to obey can be almost irresistible.

The authority effect operates in subtle ways in our everyday lives. It's the reason why people follow their doctor's advice without question, why employees carry out tasks that may seem pointless or unethical simply because their boss instructed them to, and why we defer to experts even when their expertise doesn't fully align with the issue at hand. Authority figures often carry a symbolic power that can make their words and actions seem more legitimate than they may deserve. We see titles, uniforms, and symbols of status as indicators that someone knows what is best, and we internalize their directives without critically evaluating them.

There is a duality to the authority effect. On one hand, respect for authority is necessary for the functioning of society. Without it, there would be chaos—children would not heed their parents, laws would be disregarded, and collective progress would be impossible. Authority provides order, establishes rules, and facilitates cooperation on a large scale. On the other hand, blind obedience can be dangerous. History is rife with examples of the destructive power of unchallenged authority—tyrannical governments, harmful medical practices, corporate scandals—all of which were facilitated by individuals failing to question the legitimacy or morality of the commands they were following.

Understanding the dynamics of authority helps us become more conscious of when we are obeying out of genuine respect and when we are obeying out of fear, habit, or misplaced trust. One of the key factors that makes authority so compelling is the fear of consequences. The repercussions of disobeying authority can range from minor social disapproval to severe punishment. In many cases, the fear of these consequences is enough to keep people in line, even when they know, deep down, that what they are being asked to do is wrong. The power of authority is often reinforced by the perceived risks of non-compliance—losing a job, facing legal consequences, or simply being judged by others.

Another factor that makes the authority effect so potent is the abdication of responsibility. When we follow the orders of an authority figure, we often feel that the responsibility for the outcome lies with them, not with us. This phenomenon, known as the "agentic state," allows individuals to distance themselves from the moral implications of their actions. "I was just following orders" becomes a justification, a way to rationalize behavior that might otherwise cause internal conflict. This psychological shift can make people capable of actions they would never consider if they felt fully responsible for their own choices.

However, not all obedience is blind, and not all authority is harmful. Positive authority figures—mentors, inspiring leaders, ethical experts—can guide us toward personal growth, help us develop skills, and create meaningful change in the world. The key is discerning between legitimate, constructive authority and authority that seeks to control or exploit. Developing this discernment requires critical thinking and the courage to ask questions. It requires us to challenge the notion that authority figures are infallible and to recognize that expertise does not always equate to moral or ethical correctness.

One way to navigate the authority effect is to cultivate a healthy skepticism. This does not mean rejecting authority outright, but rather approaching it with a critical mind. Ask yourself: Is this person truly qualified to make this decision? Are their directives in line with my values and ethical beliefs? What are the potential consequences of following their lead, and am I willing to accept those consequences? By questioning authority in this way, we take back some of the power that blind obedience takes from us. We become active participants in our own lives rather than passive followers.

Another strategy is to build confidence in your own judgment. Often, we defer to authority because we lack confidence in our own ability to make the right decision. By educating ourselves, seeking out diverse perspectives, and learning to trust our instincts, we can begin to rely less on external authority and more on our internal compass. This does not mean disregarding expertise—it means integrating it with our own knowledge and values to make well-rounded, informed decisions.

The authority effect is a powerful force, one that shapes our actions in ways we may not always recognize. But by understanding its roots, acknowledging its influence, and developing the tools to question and evaluate authority, we can ensure that our obedience is a choice rather than an automatic response. Authority can guide us, protect us, and help us grow—but only if we engage with it consciously, with both respect and scrutiny.

In the next chapter, we will explore the power of peer pressure—the influence of those closest to us and how the desire for acceptance can shape our actions. Peer pressure is another form of unseen influence, one that operates not through commands but through the subtle, pervasive weight of social expectations. Understanding how these forces work together is key to navigating the unseen social currents that shape our lives.

Chapter 4: Peer Pressure: The Weight of Acceptance

Peer pressure is one of the most powerful forces of social influence, particularly because it comes from those closest to us—our friends, colleagues, and social circles. Unlike authority, which relies on a perceived hierarchy, peer pressure operates on a more horizontal plane, fueled by the deep human desire for acceptance and belonging. It is the need to be liked, to fit in, and to be seen as part of the group that often pushes us to act in ways we wouldn't otherwise consider. While we may think of peer pressure as something that primarily affects adolescents, the truth is that its power persists throughout our lives, subtly shaping our behaviors and decisions.

The roots of peer pressure are tied to our evolutionary past. For our ancestors, being part of a cohesive group was crucial for survival. Being cast out from the group meant facing the dangers of the natural world alone, and this deep-seated fear of social exclusion still lingers within us. Our instinct to belong is not just emotional; it is biological, ingrained into our psyche as a survival mechanism. This is why the disapproval of peers can feel almost like a physical threat—our bodies and minds are wired to respond strongly to any indication that we might be rejected or ostracized.

Peer pressure often manifests in subtle ways. It can be as obvious as friends encouraging you to drink at a party or as insidious as the silent judgment you feel when you choose to do something different from the group. It can take the form of direct persuasion—explicit requests or dares—or indirect cues like raised eyebrows, laughter, or exclusion. The fear of being left out, of not being part of the group, creates a powerful incentive to conform, even when that conformity goes against our values or desires. This pressure often leads people to take risks, engage in behaviors they are uncomfortable with, or silence their own opinions to avoid standing out.

Adolescence is often viewed as the peak of susceptibility to peer pressure, and for good reason. Teenagers are navigating the complex process of forming their own identities, while simultaneously trying to fit in and avoid being singled out. This is a time when the opinions of friends carry enormous weight, sometimes even more than the guidance of family or authority figures. Whether it's experimenting with risky behaviors, adopting certain fashion trends, or mimicking speech patterns, the influence of peers can be incredibly strong during this developmental stage. The desire to belong can override personal judgment, leading adolescents to take actions that they later regret.

However, peer pressure does not end with adolescence. Adults are also highly susceptible to the influence of their peers, although it may manifest in different ways. In the workplace, there is often pressure to conform to the dominant culture—whether that means working late hours to prove dedication, participating in office gossip, or following along with decisions even when there are doubts about their validity. Among friends, it can mean spending money on things we don't need to keep up appearances, agreeing with opinions we don't truly hold, or engaging in behaviors that don't align with our values just to maintain social harmony. The need for acceptance is a lifelong force, one that continues to shape our actions in subtle yet significant ways.

One of the most damaging aspects of peer pressure is that it often leads us to betray ourselves. We suppress our authentic thoughts and desires to avoid conflict, discomfort, or rejection. This self-betrayal can lead to an internal dissonance—a gap between who we are and who we feel we must pretend to be in order to be accepted. Over time, this dissonance can erode self-esteem and create a lingering sense of dissatisfaction. It's difficult to feel fulfilled when the choices we make are not truly our own but are driven by the perceived expectations of others.

However, peer pressure is not always negative. It can also be a powerful force for good. Positive peer pressure can encourage us to adopt healthier habits, push us to achieve more, and support us in making beneficial changes in our lives. Surrounding ourselves with people who challenge us in constructive ways, who model positive behaviors, and who encourage us to grow can be one of the most effective ways to bring about personal improvement. The key is to recognize the difference between positive and negative pressure and to choose our associations accordingly.

Recognizing the presence of peer pressure in our lives requires self-awareness. It involves being honest with ourselves about why we are making certain choices—are we doing this because it aligns with our values, or are we doing it because we feel pressured by those around us? Asking this question can help us identify when we are being influenced in ways that do not serve our best interests. It's also important to cultivate the courage to stand apart when necessary. This means being willing to accept that we may not always fit in, that we may face disapproval, and that not everyone will agree with our choices.

One of the most effective ways to resist negative peer pressure is to develop a strong sense of self. When we are clear about our values, our goals, and who we want to be, we are less likely to be swayed by the opinions of others. Building this internal foundation takes time and introspection, but it is the best defense against the subtle forces of peer influence. It also helps to seek out environments that align with our values—communities, workplaces, and friendships where individuality is respected and positive behaviors are encouraged. By choosing our associations carefully, we can create a network of peers who uplift rather than pressure us into conformity.

Another strategy for dealing with peer pressure is to practice assertiveness. Being assertive does not mean being confrontational; it means expressing your thoughts, feelings, and needs honestly and respectfully. When faced with peer pressure, assertiveness allows you to set boundaries without alienating others. It is the skill of saying "no" in a way that is firm but not aggressive, of expressing dissent without belittling others. Assertiveness empowers us to navigate social dynamics with integrity, maintaining our own sense of self while still being part of the group.

Ultimately, peer pressure is about the balance between individuality and belonging. It is natural to want to fit in, to be accepted, and to feel a sense of connection with those around us. But true belonging cannot come at the cost of our authentic selves. It is only when we are able to be who we truly are, without fear of rejection, that we can experience real connection. The challenge is to find the courage to be ourselves, even when the pressure to conform feels overwhelming, and to surround ourselves with those who celebrate our uniqueness rather than demand our conformity.

In the next chapter, we will turn our attention to the influence of social media—the digital age's amplifier of peer pressure and the unseen forces that shape our behavior. We will explore how algorithms, influencers, and online communities amplify the pull of social influence, and how we can navigate these forces in a way that allows us to stay true to ourselves. Understanding peer pressure is the first step, but in a world increasingly dominated by digital interaction, learning how to manage influence online is crucial to maintaining autonomy in our decisions and actions.

Chapter 5: Social Media and the Amplification of Influence

Social media has become an omnipresent part of our daily lives, profoundly shaping the way we interact, communicate, and even perceive ourselves. It is a powerful amplifier of influence, magnifying both the positive and negative forces that shape our behavior. Unlike traditional forms of peer pressure and authority, social media operates in a borderless space, where algorithms, influencers, and an endless stream of curated content create an environment of constant comparison and influence. In this chapter, we will explore how social media intensifies social influence, how it impacts our sense of identity, and how we can navigate this digital landscape without losing our sense of self.

One of the key ways in which social media amplifies influence is through the constant exposure to curated versions of other people's lives. The images and stories that populate our feeds are not random snapshots—they are carefully selected and edited to present an idealized version of reality. Whether it is a photo of a perfect vacation, a beautifully plated meal, or a seemingly effortless achievement, the content we see on social media is designed to elicit a reaction, often one of admiration or envy. This creates a cycle of comparison, where we measure our own lives against the highlight reels of others, often to our own detriment. The pressure to keep up, to present a similarly perfect image, can lead to feelings of inadequacy, anxiety, and a distorted sense of self-worth.

Algorithms play a significant role in shaping the content we see and, by extension, the beliefs and behaviors we adopt. Social media platforms are designed to maximize user engagement, which means that the content we are shown is not just based on our interests but also on what will keep us scrolling. Algorithms prioritize content that elicits strong emotional responses—whether positive or negative—because these responses drive interaction. This can create echo chambers, where we are repeatedly exposed to the same ideas, opinions, and values, reinforcing our existing beliefs and limiting our exposure to diverse perspectives. The influence of algorithms is subtle but powerful, guiding our attention and shaping our worldview without us even realizing it.

The rise of influencers has also changed the dynamics of social influence. Influencers are individuals who have built significant followings on social media platforms, and their opinions, endorsements, and lifestyles carry considerable weight with their audiences. Unlike traditional celebrities, influencers often present themselves as more relatable, positioning themselves as friends or peers rather than unattainable figures. This perceived relatability makes their influence even more potent, as followers may feel a personal connection to them. Whether it is promoting a product, a lifestyle, or a belief, influencers have the power to shape the behaviors and attitudes of millions, often blurring the line between authentic recommendations and paid promotions.

The impact of social media on self-esteem and identity is profound. The validation that comes from likes, comments, and shares can become addictive, creating a feedback loop where our sense of self-worth becomes tied to online approval. The desire for validation can lead us to curate our own lives in ways that are not authentic, presenting only the parts of ourselves that we believe will be well-received by others. This can create a disconnect between our online persona and our real selves, leading to feelings of emptiness and a lack of genuine connection. The constant need to present a perfect image can also contribute to stress, as we strive to meet unrealistic standards set by the curated lives of others.

However, social media is not inherently negative. It has the potential to connect us with like-minded individuals, to provide support, and to amplify positive messages. It can be a platform for advocacy, education, and community-building. The key to navigating social media in a healthy way is to approach it with awareness and intention. Recognizing that what we see online is not an accurate representation of reality is crucial to mitigating the negative effects of comparison. It is also important to be mindful of the content we consume and the impact it has on our mental and emotional well-being. Curating our feeds to include positive, diverse, and uplifting content can help counterbalance the negative aspects of social media.

One strategy for maintaining a healthy relationship with social media is to set boundaries. This can mean limiting the amount of time spent on social media, unfollowing accounts that make us feel inadequate, or taking breaks when it becomes overwhelming. It is also helpful to cultivate a sense of self-worth that is independent of online validation. This means finding fulfillment in real-life relationships, achievements, and experiences rather than relying on likes and comments to feel valued. Building this internal sense of self-worth can help us engage with social media in a way that is less about seeking approval and more about genuine connection and expression.

Another important aspect of navigating social media is developing critical thinking skills. The content we see online is often designed to influence us, whether it is to buy a product, adopt a trend, or support a particular viewpoint. By approaching social media with a critical eye—questioning the motivations behind the content, recognizing sponsored posts, and being aware of the ways in which algorithms shape our experience—we can make more informed decisions about what we engage with and how it affects us. Critical thinking allows us to be active participants in our social media experience rather than passive consumers.

Social media has fundamentally changed the way we experience influence. It has amplified the reach and power of social forces, making it more important than ever to understand how these forces operate and how they affect us. By approaching social media with awareness, setting healthy boundaries, and cultivating a strong sense of self-worth, we can navigate this digital landscape without losing sight of who we are. The goal is not to reject social media entirely, but to engage with it in a way that enhances rather than diminishes our well-being.

In the next chapter, we will explore the subtle power of cultural norms—how the invisible rules of our culture shape our beliefs and behaviors, often without us even realizing it. Understanding the influence of cultural norms is key to recognizing the forces that guide our actions and learning how to make choices that are truly our own.

Chapter 6: The Subtle Power of Cultural Norms

Cultural norms are the invisible rules that dictate how we live, often without us even realizing it. They shape our beliefs, values, behaviors, and even the way we perceive the world. These norms are passed down through generations, embedded in our customs, traditions, language, and the everyday interactions we often take for granted. Unlike peer pressure or authority, which can be more overt, cultural norms operate quietly in the background, providing a framework for what is considered acceptable or desirable. This chapter explores how these unseen forces influence our lives and how we can become more aware of their impact in order to make conscious choices about which norms we want to follow and which we might want to challenge.

Cultural norms provide a sense of order and stability. They create a shared understanding of how people should behave, what is valued, and what is expected in different situations. This shared understanding is crucial for social cohesion; it allows individuals within a community to predict how others will behave and to interact with a sense of mutual respect and familiarity. For example, norms around politeness, respect for elders, or the importance of family help ensure that people coexist harmoniously. These norms help to create a sense of belonging, as adhering to them signals that we are part of a community, that we share its values and contribute to its stability.

However, the power of cultural norms can also be limiting. Because these norms are so deeply ingrained, they can restrict individuality, stifle creativity, and prevent people from questioning the status quo. We often accept cultural norms without critically examining them, assuming that the way things are is the way they must be. This unquestioning acceptance can lead to the perpetuation of harmful beliefs and practices, from gender roles that limit individual potential to societal expectations that define what success looks like. Cultural norms dictate everything from how we dress to how we express emotion, to the kinds of careers we believe are available to us. The invisible nature of these influences makes them particularly powerful because we rarely stop to consider where they come from or why we follow them.

Take, for example, norms surrounding gender roles. In many cultures, there are specific expectations about how men and women should behave—how they should dress, the kinds of work they should do, and the roles they should play within a family. These expectations are not innate; they are learned through years of conditioning, reinforced by media, education, and the behavior of those around us. For many people, stepping outside of these prescribed roles can lead to social disapproval, isolation, or even punishment. The power of cultural norms lies in their ability to make us feel that deviation is dangerous, that to be different is to be wrong. This creates an environment where many individuals suppress their true selves to avoid conflict, shame, or exclusion.

Cultural norms also influence how we perceive success and happiness. In some societies, success is equated with financial wealth, career achievements, and social status. People are conditioned to believe that the only path to a fulfilling life is through material prosperity, even if pursuing that path comes at the expense of personal relationships, mental health, or genuine happiness. These norms can create immense pressure, leading individuals to chase goals that do not align with their true desires, simply because they are following a culturally defined script for what it means to be successful. The cost of adhering to these norms can be high—burnout, dissatisfaction, and a deep sense of unfulfillment are common consequences of pursuing goals that do not resonate with one's authentic self.

The influence of cultural norms is also evident in how we approach relationships. Norms dictate not only who we should love but also how we should express that love. In some cultures, expressions of affection are open and celebrated, while in others, they are more reserved. Norms determine the roles that individuals play within a relationship, often assigning specific duties and expectations based on gender or social standing. These norms can make it difficult for people to form relationships that are equitable and based on true partnership, rather than on societal expectations. The pressure to conform to these norms can lead to relationships that are more about meeting societal standards than about genuine connection and mutual fulfillment.

One of the most challenging aspects of cultural norms is that they are so deeply embedded that we often internalize them as personal beliefs. We may think we are acting out of our own free will, when in fact, we are following a set of rules that have been imposed on us by the culture we were born into. This internalization makes it difficult to recognize when we are being influenced. The fear of stepping outside of these norms, of being judged or ostracized, can keep us from questioning their validity or from seeking a path that is more aligned with our personal values and desires.

However, cultural norms are not immutable. They change over time, often as a result of individuals who are willing to challenge them. Social movements, shifts in collective consciousness, and the courage of those who dare to be different all contribute to the evolution of cultural norms. Women entering the workforce, the fight for LGBTQ+ rights, the growing emphasis on mental health—all of these are examples of how cultural norms can shift when people refuse to accept them as unchangeable truths. Change begins with awareness—with recognizing that the norms we live by are not laws of nature but constructs that can be questioned and reshaped.

To navigate the subtle power of cultural norms, it is essential to develop cultural awareness. This means taking the time to reflect on the beliefs and values we hold and asking ourselves where they come from. Are they truly our own, or are they the result of conditioning? Do they serve us, or do they limit us? This kind of introspection allows us to differentiate between the norms that align with our personal values and those that do not. It empowers us to make conscious choices about which norms to follow, which to challenge, and which to redefine for ourselves.

Another important aspect of navigating cultural norms is learning to respect differences without judgment. Just as we are shaped by our culture, so are others. What seems strange or wrong to us may be perfectly normal and meaningful to someone else. Developing an understanding of different cultural norms and the reasons behind them can help us to be more open-minded and compassionate. It also allows us to see that there are many different ways to live a meaningful and fulfilling life—ways that may differ from the norms we were taught but are no less valid.

The subtle power of cultural norms is a testament to the influence of the unseen forces that shape our lives. By becoming aware of these norms, questioning their origins, and consciously choosing which ones to follow, we can begin to live more authentically. We can create lives that reflect our true selves rather than the expectations imposed upon us by others.

This process is not always easy—it often involves stepping outside of comfort zones, facing criticism, and challenging long-held beliefs. But it is the only way to break free from the invisible constraints that limit our potential and to create a life that is truly our own.

In the next chapter, we will examine the impact of unspoken cues—body language and social signals—that influence our behavior in ways we might not even realize. These cues are part of the nonverbal communication that shapes our interactions and can have a powerful effect on how we perceive others and how we are perceived in return. Understanding these cues is essential for navigating the complexities of human interaction and for becoming more attuned to the subtle forces at play in our social environments.

Chapter 7: The Impact of Unspoken Cues: Body Language and Social Signals

Communication is not limited to the words we speak. In fact, much of the communication that takes place between people is nonverbal, conveyed through body language, facial expressions, tone of voice, and other unspoken cues. These signals are powerful—they shape our interactions, influence our perceptions, and often dictate how we respond to others. Unlike verbal language, which can be deliberate and controlled, nonverbal communication is often automatic, revealing what we truly feel even when we try to hide it. In this chapter, we explore the impact of unspoken cues, how they influence our social interactions, and how becoming aware of these signals can enhance our understanding of the subtle dynamics at play in our relationships.

Body language is one of the most significant aspects of nonverbal communication. The way we stand, the gestures we use, our posture, and even the amount of space we maintain between ourselves and others can all convey messages that are sometimes more powerful than words. For example, crossed arms might signal defensiveness, while an open posture can convey approachability and openness. A firm handshake can suggest confidence, while avoiding eye contact can be interpreted as a lack of interest or even deceit. These cues are often interpreted instinctively, without conscious thought, and they can shape how others perceive us in a matter of seconds.

Facial expressions are another crucial element of nonverbal communication. The human face is capable of conveying a vast range of emotions, often with just subtle shifts in muscle movement. A raised eyebrow, a slight frown, or a genuine smile can convey approval, skepticism, anger, or warmth without a single word being spoken. Facial expressions are universal in many ways; emotions like happiness, sadness, fear, and anger are expressed similarly across cultures. This universality allows us to communicate and understand emotions even when language barriers exist. However, cultural differences can still play a role in how these expressions are used and interpreted, which means that understanding context is essential for accurate interpretation.

Tone of voice, or paralinguistics, also plays a critical role in nonverbal communication. The same words can carry entirely different meanings depending on how they are said. Tone can convey sarcasm, sincerity, excitement, or boredom. A raised pitch might indicate surprise, while a slow, deliberate tone could suggest seriousness or even irritation. The emotional undertone of our speech often communicates more than the words themselves, and it is this quality that allows listeners to discern the true intent behind what is being said. The mismatch between tone and content—like saying "I'm fine" in a clearly frustrated voice—can often reveal underlying emotions that the speaker might not want to admit openly.

Nonverbal cues are powerful because they provide a glimpse into our genuine feelings and intentions. Unlike verbal language, which can be carefully constructed, nonverbal communication often leaks the truth of what we are experiencing internally. This is why people can sometimes tell when someone is lying—the words may be convincing, but the body language, facial expressions, or tone of voice might betray the real emotion underneath. Studies have shown that when there is a discrepancy between verbal and nonverbal messages, people tend to trust the nonverbal cues more. This instinct to trust nonverbal signals comes from our evolutionary past, where accurately interpreting others' intentions could mean the difference between survival and danger.

The ability to read and interpret unspoken cues is an essential social skill, one that affects everything from our personal relationships to our professional interactions. In social situations, being attuned to nonverbal signals allows us to gauge the mood of others, to understand their level of interest, comfort, or engagement, and to adjust our behavior accordingly. For example, noticing that someone is leaning away or has their arms crossed might prompt us to change the topic of conversation or to give them more personal space. On the other hand, recognizing signs of engagement—like leaning in, nodding, and maintaining eye contact—can encourage us to continue what we are doing. These cues help us navigate social dynamics more effectively, fostering better understanding and connection.

In the professional world, nonverbal communication can be just as important as verbal communication, if not more so. During job interviews, meetings, or negotiations, body language and facial expressions can convey confidence, competence, and openness—or, conversely, insecurity, disinterest, or hostility. Understanding the nonverbal cues of others can provide valuable insights into their thoughts and feelings, which can be especially useful in negotiations or conflict resolution. Similarly, being aware of our own nonverbal signals allows us to project the image we want to convey, helping us build trust, credibility, and positive rapport with colleagues and clients.

However, it is important to remember that nonverbal cues are not always easy to interpret. Context matters—a gesture or expression that means one thing in a particular setting might mean something entirely different in another. Cultural differences also play a significant role in how nonverbal communication is used and understood. For instance, maintaining eye contact is seen as a sign of confidence and honesty in some cultures, while in others, it can be perceived as disrespectful or confrontational. Understanding these cultural nuances is crucial for effective communication, particularly in a diverse or multicultural environment.

To navigate the complex world of nonverbal communication, it is helpful to cultivate mindfulness and observation skills. Paying attention to the body language of others, noting their facial expressions, and listening not just to their words but also to the tone of their voice can provide valuable insights into what they are truly feeling. It is also important to be mindful of our own nonverbal signals. Are we crossing our arms in a way that might suggest defensiveness? Is our tone of voice conveying frustration when we mean to be supportive? By becoming more aware of the unspoken cues we give and receive, we can enhance our ability to communicate effectively and authentically.

Another key aspect of understanding unspoken cues is learning to align our verbal and nonverbal messages. Consistency between what we say and how we say it is crucial for building trust and credibility. When our words match our body language, facial expressions, and tone of voice, we are seen as more genuine and trustworthy. This alignment is especially important in relationships, where mixed messages can lead to misunderstandings and conflicts. By ensuring that our nonverbal communication supports our verbal intent, we can create clearer, more meaningful connections with others.

The impact of unspoken cues on our social interactions cannot be overstated. They are the foundation of our ability to connect, to empathize, and to understand each other beyond the surface level. By paying attention to these cues, both in ourselves and in others, we can navigate social situations with greater ease, build stronger relationships, and communicate more effectively. In a world where so much of our interaction is filtered through screens and digital devices, the ability to understand and interpret nonverbal signals is more valuable than ever—it is what allows us to maintain genuine human connection in an increasingly virtual world.

In the next chapter, we will explore the phenomenon of the echo chamber effect—how our desire for social harmony and our tendency toward confirmation bias can lead to groupthink and the reinforcement of existing beliefs. Understanding how these forces work is essential for breaking free from the cycle of unquestioned opinions and learning to think more critically about the information we encounter.

Chapter 8: The Echo Chamber Effect: Confirmation Bias and Groupthink

In an increasingly interconnected world, the phenomenon of echo chambers has become a defining feature of modern social dynamics. An echo chamber is created when we surround ourselves with people, information, and opinions that align with our existing beliefs, filtering out anything that challenges or contradicts them. It is a natural byproduct of our desire for certainty and social harmony, and it is often reinforced by the very tools we use to connect—social media algorithms, curated news feeds, and like-minded social circles. This chapter delves into the power of the echo chamber effect, how it fosters confirmation bias, and the dangers of groupthink, while also providing strategies for breaking free from these unseen forces and fostering critical thinking.

The echo chamber effect begins with a very human tendency: the need for validation. We seek out information that confirms what we already believe because it feels good—it reassures us that we are right, that our worldview is accurate, and that we belong to a community of like-minded individuals. This process is known as confirmation bias, and it is one of the most pervasive cognitive biases in human psychology. Confirmation bias leads us to favor information that supports our beliefs while disregarding or downplaying evidence that contradicts them. It is why we often ignore facts that make us uncomfortable, why we are quick to dismiss opposing viewpoints, and why we find it so difficult to change our minds even in the face of new evidence.

Social media platforms and search engines amplify confirmation bias by providing us with content that aligns with our interests and beliefs. Algorithms are designed to maximize engagement, which means showing us more of what we like and less of what might challenge us. This creates a self-reinforcing cycle, where we are continually exposed to ideas that echo our own, making our beliefs feel more validated and more universally accepted than they actually are. The more we engage with content that confirms our views, the less likely we are to encounter opposing perspectives, and the more insulated our worldview becomes.

This isolation can make it increasingly difficult to have productive conversations with those who see the world differently, as we come to perceive opposing viewpoints as not just incorrect, but fundamentally irrational or even threatening.

Groupthink is another consequence of the echo chamber effect, particularly within closely-knit groups where social cohesion is prioritized over critical evaluation. Groupthink occurs when the desire for harmony or conformity within a group leads to poor decision-making. Members of the group suppress dissenting opinions, avoid conflict, and often come to an uncritical consensus, even when there are clear warning signs that the group's decision may be flawed. Groupthink can lead to disastrous outcomes—historical examples like the Bay of Pigs invasion or the Challenger space shuttle disaster illustrate how groupthink can prevent individuals from speaking up, even when they know something is wrong.

The problem with echo chambers and groupthink is that they create an illusion of consensus and certainty. When everyone around us shares our beliefs, it becomes easy to assume that our perspective is not only right but also the only reasonable one. This illusion can lead to polarization, where differing groups become more extreme in their views, less willing to listen to each other, and more likely to dismiss or demonize opposing perspectives. The more polarized we become, the harder it is to find common ground, and the more fragmented our societies become. This fragmentation weakens our ability to solve collective problems, as we become more focused on defending our positions than on understanding each other or finding solutions.

Breaking free from the echo chamber effect requires conscious effort and a willingness to engage with discomfort. It begins with recognizing our own biases—the understanding that we all have a tendency to favor information that makes us feel comfortable and validated. Once we acknowledge this, we can take steps to seek out diverse perspectives, to question our assumptions, and to expose ourselves to viewpoints that challenge us. This does not mean that we have to agree with everything we read or hear, but it does mean approaching differing opinions with curiosity rather than hostility. The goal is not to change our beliefs with every new piece of information, but to be open to the possibility that we might be wrong, and to understand why others might see things differently.

Cultivating critical thinking skills is another essential strategy for counteracting the effects of echo chambers and groupthink. Critical thinking involves analyzing information objectively, evaluating the credibility of sources, and questioning whether our conclusions are supported by evidence. It requires us to ask difficult questions: Why do I believe this? What evidence supports it? What evidence contradicts it? Where does my information come from, and is it reliable? Developing these skills allows us to step back from the automatic acceptance of information and to make more informed, deliberate decisions.

It is also helpful to diversify our information sources. Instead of relying solely on social media or a single news outlet, we can seek out multiple perspectives, particularly those that challenge our views. Reading broadly, listening to experts with different backgrounds, and engaging in conversations with people who see the world differently can help us break out of the echo chamber. This does not mean passively accepting every viewpoint, but rather engaging critically and respectfully, recognizing that differing perspectives can provide valuable insights, even if we ultimately disagree.

Another strategy for avoiding groupthink is to foster environments where dissent is encouraged and valued. In group settings, whether in a workplace, community, or social circle, it is important to create a culture where people feel comfortable expressing different opinions without fear of ridicule or exclusion. This can be achieved by actively inviting dissenting views, playing "devil's advocate," and emphasizing that disagreement is a healthy part of the decision-making process. Leaders, in particular, play a crucial role in setting this tone—by modeling openness to criticism and valuing diverse input, they can help prevent the conformity that leads to poor group decisions.

The echo chamber effect and the tendency toward groupthink are natural byproducts of our social nature. We are wired to seek connection, validation, and harmony, but these instincts can also lead us into intellectual isolation and prevent us from seeing the full complexity of the world. By recognizing these tendencies, questioning our assumptions, and actively seeking out diverse perspectives, we can break free from the confines of our echo chambers and contribute to a more open, understanding, and connected society.

In the next chapter, we will explore the concept of manipulation—how unseen social forces are sometimes used deliberately to influence our decisions and behaviors, often without our awareness. Understanding the tactics of manipulation is essential for protecting our autonomy and making choices that truly reflect our values and beliefs.

Chapter 9: Recognizing and Resisting Manipulation

Manipulation is one of the most insidious forms of social influence—an unseen force that can shape our decisions, often without our awareness. Unlike other forms of influence, which may arise naturally from our desire to belong or fit in, manipulation is deliberate. It is a calculated effort by individuals, groups, or institutions to influence our behavior for their own benefit, often at the expense of our autonomy. Understanding the tactics of manipulation is essential for protecting ourselves, making informed decisions, and ensuring that our actions reflect our true values rather than the hidden agendas of others. In this chapter, we will explore how manipulation operates, the psychological principles behind it, and how we can resist it effectively.

Manipulation often preys on our vulnerabilities—our emotions, fears, desires, and need for validation. It can take many forms, from the subtle use of language to evoke an emotional response to the more overt use of threats or deception. One of the most common tactics is emotional manipulation, which involves triggering strong feelings like guilt, fear, or love to influence behavior. Advertisers, for example, often use emotionally charged imagery or narratives to create a sense of urgency or desire—think of charity ads that show suffering children or luxury car commercials that appeal to our desire for status. The goal is to bypass rational thought and evoke an emotional reaction that leads us to act in ways that benefit the manipulator.

Another common tactic of manipulation is the use of scarcity. The idea of scarcity—whether real or perceived—creates a sense of urgency, making us feel that we need to act quickly to avoid missing out. This tactic is often used in sales and marketing, with phrases like "limited time offer" or "only a few items left" designed to make us believe that we need to make an immediate decision. The fear of missing out, or FOMO, can cloud our judgment, leading us to make choices that we might not otherwise consider if we took the time to think them through logically. Scarcity taps into our primal fear of losing an opportunity, pushing us to act impulsively rather than thoughtfully.

Social proof is another powerful tool used in manipulation. We are social creatures, and we tend to look to others for cues on how to behave, especially in situations where we are uncertain. Manipulators often exploit this tendency by creating the illusion of widespread approval or consensus. For example, advertisements that feature testimonials or claim that a product is "the number one choice" of consumers are leveraging social proof to influence our decisions. The idea is that if so many people are choosing something, it must be good, and we would be wise to follow their lead. Social proof can be an effective way of persuading us to act without fully considering whether the action is right for us.

Authority is another lever frequently used by manipulators. As discussed in earlier chapters, we are conditioned to respect authority figures and often assume that they know what is best. This makes us vulnerable to manipulation by those who present themselves as experts or wield symbols of authority, such as uniforms, titles, or certifications. A financial advisor, for instance, might use their credentials to convince clients to invest in products that are not in their best interest but serve the advisor's financial gain. The use of authority in manipulation works because it taps into our instinct to defer to those we perceive as knowledgeable or powerful, often bypassing our own critical thinking.

The use of guilt and obligation is another common manipulation tactic. Guilt is a powerful motivator, and manipulators often use it to get what they want. This can happen in personal relationships, where someone might imply that we owe them something because of what they have done for us, or in sales, where a "free gift" is given with the expectation that we will then feel obligated to make a purchase. This tactic works by exploiting our sense of fairness and reciprocity—we feel that we must give something in return, even if we had no intention of doing so initially. Manipulators understand that most people want to be seen as fair and kind, and they use this to push us into actions that benefit them.

Recognizing manipulation requires a high level of self-awareness and a willingness to question both our own reactions and the motivations of others. One of the first steps in resisting manipulation is to recognize the emotional triggers being used against us. When we feel a sudden rush of fear, excitement, guilt, or urgency, it is helpful to pause and ask ourselves whether these emotions are being deliberately provoked. Are we being pushed to make a decision before we have had time to think it through? Are we acting out of fear of missing out or because we genuinely believe it is the right choice? By identifying these emotional triggers, we can create space to evaluate the situation more rationally.

Another important strategy for resisting manipulation is to cultivate critical thinking skills. This means questioning the information we are presented with, considering the source, and evaluating whether there might be an ulterior motive. For example, if someone is presenting themselves as an authority, it is worth considering whether they truly have the expertise they claim, and whether they might have something to gain from influencing our decision. Critical thinking allows us to see beyond the surface of what is being presented to us and to evaluate the underlying motivations of those who seek to influence us.

Setting clear boundaries is also crucial for resisting manipulation, particularly in personal relationships. Manipulators often push against boundaries, using guilt, obligation, or emotional appeals to get what they want. By being clear about our own limits—what we are willing to do and what we are not—we can protect ourselves from being coerced into actions that do not serve our best interests. This requires confidence and assertiveness, as well as the understanding that we have the right to say no, even if it disappoints others. Boundaries are a way of asserting our autonomy, of making it clear that we are in control of our own choices.

It is also helpful to practice emotional detachment when evaluating a situation where manipulation might be at play. This does not mean being cold or unfeeling, but rather taking a step back to assess the situation logically rather than emotionally. Manipulators rely on strong emotional responses to override rational thought. By taking a moment to detach and analyze the situation from a more objective perspective, we can make decisions that are based on our values and best interests rather than on the manipulator's agenda.

Manipulation is a powerful form of influence because it often goes unnoticed until after the fact. By understanding the tactics that manipulators use—emotional triggers, scarcity, social proof, authority, guilt, and obligation—we can become more vigilant and better equipped to resist these influences. The goal is not to become distrustful of everyone we encounter, but to develop the awareness and critical thinking skills necessary to protect our autonomy. Manipulation thrives in the absence of awareness; by shining a light on these tactics, we take the first step toward reclaiming control over our own decisions and actions.

In the next chapter, we will explore how we can take back control from all of these unseen social forces, using strategies for conscious decision-making that align with our values and true desires. Understanding the nature of influence is only the beginning—true empowerment comes from learning how to navigate these forces with clarity and intention, ensuring that our actions are genuinely our own.

Chapter 10: Taking Back Control: Strategies for Conscious Decision-Making

Understanding the unseen social forces that influence us is only the first step toward reclaiming our autonomy. True empowerment comes not just from recognizing these forces but from actively taking steps to counteract them and to make decisions that align with our own values and desires. In this chapter, we explore practical strategies for conscious decision-making—ways to live intentionally and navigate the complex landscape of influence without losing sight of who we are. These strategies are designed to help us move beyond the automatic responses that often characterize our behavior, allowing us to act in ways that are truly reflective of our authentic selves.

One of the most powerful tools for taking back control is cultivating self-awareness. Self-awareness is the foundation of all conscious decision-making. It involves understanding our own thoughts, emotions, motivations, and behaviors, as well as recognizing the influences that shape them. By developing self-awareness, we can identify when we are acting out of habit, fear, or social pressure rather than from genuine intent. This awareness creates the space needed to pause, reflect, and choose how to respond, rather than simply reacting. Journaling, mindfulness meditation, and reflective practices are all effective ways to enhance self-awareness. By regularly examining our thoughts and actions, we can begin to see patterns that reveal where we are being influenced and where we might want to make a change.

Another important strategy for conscious decision-making is setting clear personal values. Our values are the guiding principles that help us determine what is truly important to us—what we stand for, what we aspire to, and what kind of life we want to lead. When we are clear about our values, it becomes easier to make decisions that are in alignment with who we are, even when faced with external pressures. For example, if we value honesty, we are less likely to be swayed by social pressure to act deceitfully, even if it might seem advantageous in the short term. Setting values is not about rigidly adhering to a set of rules but about having a compass that helps us navigate complex situations with integrity and authenticity.

Critical thinking is another key component of conscious decision-making. The ability to evaluate information objectively, question assumptions, and consider different perspectives allows us to make informed choices rather than relying on automatic or emotionally-driven reactions. Critical thinking requires us to ask questions: Is this information credible? What is the source? What are the potential biases at play? What are the consequences of this decision, and who stands to benefit? By developing the habit of questioning both the information we receive and the motivations behind it, we can avoid being manipulated or swayed by misleading narratives. Critical thinking empowers us to be active participants in our own lives, making decisions that are grounded in reason and evidence rather than in impulse or coercion.

Mindfulness is another powerful strategy for taking back control. Mindfulness is the practice of being present in the moment, fully aware of our thoughts, emotions, and surroundings without judgment. When we are mindful, we are less likely to be caught up in automatic behaviors or influenced by unconscious biases. Mindfulness allows us to observe our thoughts and feelings without immediately reacting to them, giving us the opportunity to choose how we want to respond. This is especially important when faced with strong emotions or social pressures, which can easily lead us to act in ways that do not reflect our true intentions. By practicing mindfulness, we can cultivate a greater sense of control over our actions, making decisions that are deliberate and in line with our values.

Setting boundaries is also essential for conscious decision-making. Boundaries are the limits we set for ourselves in order to protect our well-being and maintain control over our lives. They help us define what is acceptable and what is not, allowing us to interact with others in a way that respects our needs and values. Setting boundaries can be particularly important when dealing with manipulative individuals or situations where we feel pressured to act against our best interests. It requires assertiveness—the ability to express our needs and desires clearly and confidently without infringing on the rights of others. By setting and maintaining healthy boundaries, we create an environment in which we can make decisions that are true to ourselves, free from undue influence.

Surrounding ourselves with supportive, like-minded individuals is another effective way to foster conscious decision-making. The people we spend time with have a significant impact on our thoughts, behaviors, and attitudes. By building relationships with those who respect our values, encourage our growth, and challenge us in constructive ways, we create a network of support that reinforces our ability to make independent decisions. Positive social environments can counterbalance the negative influences we encounter, providing us with the strength and confidence to stay true to ourselves. It is also important to recognize that we have the power to choose our associations—if certain relationships are consistently undermining our well-being or pressuring us to act in ways that do not align with our values, it may be necessary to distance ourselves from those influences.

Another strategy for conscious decision-making is practicing delayed decision-making. When faced with a decision, particularly one that evokes a strong emotional response or feels pressured, it can be helpful to take a step back and give ourselves time to reflect. The pressure to act immediately, whether due to scarcity tactics, emotional appeals, or social pressure, can lead to impulsive choices that we later regret. By taking time to consider our options, evaluate the consequences, and consult our values, we can make decisions that are more thoughtful and aligned with our long-term goals. Practicing delayed decision-making helps us move away from reactive behaviors and towards a more intentional, deliberate approach to our actions.

Lastly, embracing the concept of personal responsibility is crucial for taking back control. Personal responsibility means recognizing that, while we may be influenced by external forces, we ultimately have the power to choose how we respond. It involves taking ownership of our decisions, acknowledging both the positive and negative outcomes, and learning from our experiences. When we take responsibility for our actions, we move away from a victim mindset—where we feel powerless in the face of external influences—and towards an empowered mindset, where we see ourselves as active agents capable of shaping our own lives. Personal responsibility is about understanding that, while we cannot always control the circumstances we face, we can control how we respond to them.

Taking back control from unseen social forces is not about rejecting influence entirely—it is about becoming aware of the influences that shape us and making deliberate choices about which ones to accept and which to resist. It is about cultivating the skills and mindset needed to navigate a complex social world with integrity, clarity, and autonomy. By developing self-awareness, setting personal values, practicing critical thinking, cultivating mindfulness, setting boundaries, surrounding ourselves with positive influences, delaying decisions, and embracing personal responsibility, we can take back control of our lives and make decisions that are truly our own.

In the final chapter, we will reflect on what it means to live at the intersection of influence and autonomy—to embrace the power of connection without losing ourselves in the process. We will explore how understanding and navigating these unseen social forces can lead to a richer, more authentic, and more fulfilling life.

Conclusion

At the core of the human experience is the delicate dance between influence and autonomy. To live authentically in a world that constantly pulls us in different directions requires both awareness and courage. We are not isolated beings; we are shaped by those around us, by our culture, by our experiences. And that's not a weakness—it's a testament to our interconnectedness, our ability to learn, to grow, and to adapt. But within that interconnectedness lies the opportunity to choose how we respond, to decide which influences we will allow to shape us, and which we will resist.

Living at the intersection of influence and autonomy means embracing the fact that we are part of something bigger, while also honoring the individuality that makes each of us unique. It means understanding that influence is not inherently good or bad—it's how we engage with it that defines our lives. It's about being open to new ideas, yet grounded in our values. It's about recognizing manipulation, resisting undue pressure, and setting boundaries where needed—all while allowing ourselves the vulnerability to connect, to belong, and to be human.

There is power in understanding the unseen forces that shape our actions. By becoming conscious of these forces, we transform from passive participants to active creators of our own lives. We take back control—not by cutting ourselves off from the world, but by engaging with it more fully, more deliberately, and more authentically. It is in this balance—between influence and autonomy, connection and independence—that we find true fulfillment.

End Note

The journey to reclaiming your autonomy is not a one-time decision—it's a continuous process. It's about showing up every day, willing to question, to reflect, and to make conscious choices. There will be times when you falter, when the pull of influence feels too strong, when you find yourself swayed by forces you thought you had overcome. That's part of being human. What matters is that you keep coming back to yourself, keep asking the questions that matter, and keep choosing to live a life that is truly your own.

You are not alone in this journey. Every one of us is navigating the same complex web of influences, trying to find our way, to live with meaning, and to connect without losing ourselves. Together, we can create a world where influence is a force for growth, not control—where autonomy is celebrated, not stifled. It starts with awareness, it grows with practice, and it becomes a way of life.

— JD Arden